Air Fryer Dessert Breakfast Cookbook

To My Family, All My Friends And All My Readers
Loren Allen

Loren Allen

© Copyright 2021 by Loren Allen - All rights reserved. The following Book is reproduced below with the goal of providing information that is as accurate and reliable as possible. Regardless, purchasing this Book can be seen as consent to the fact that both the publisher and the author of this book are in no way experts on the topics discussed within and that any recommendations or suggestions that are made herein are for entertainment purposes only. Professionals should be consulted as needed prior to undertaking any of the action endorsed herein. This declaration is deemed fair and valid by both the American Bar Association and the Committee of Publishers Association and is legally binding throughout the United States. Furthermore, the transmission, duplication, or reproduction of any of the following work including specific information will be considered an illegal act irrespective of if it is done electronically or in print. This extends to creating a secondary or tertiary copy of the work or a recorded copy and is only allowed with the express written consent from the Publisher. All additional right reserved. The information in the following pages is broadly considered a truthful and accurate account of facts and as such, any inattention, use, or misuse of the information in question by the reader will render any resulting actions solely under their purview. There are no scenarios in which the publisher or the original author of this work can be in any fashion deemed liable for any hardship or damages that may befall them after undertaking information described herein

Additionally, the information in the following pages is intended only for informational purposes and should thus be thought of as universal. As befitting its nature, it is presented without assurance regarding its prolonged validity or interim quality. Trademarks that are mentioned are done without written consent and can in no way be considered an endorsement from the trademark holder.

Table Of Contents

Introduction	8
The truth is...	10
My Story	12
Why You Shoul Buy An Air Fryer or...a Vortex	17
Like Michelangelo...	19
DO YOU WANT TO KNOW WHY BREAKFAST, WELL I WOULD SAY ALSO BREAKFAST?	20
WHAT IS THIS BOOK ABOUT?	20
WHO IS IT FOR?	20
WHAT'S INSIDE?	21
Let's Start Creating!	22
Lemon-Raspberry Muffins	23
Fluffy Brownies Muffins	25
Peanut Butter Custard	27
Cinnamon Cheesecake Bars	29
Butter Cake	31
Oatmeal Cake	33
Shortbread Fingers	35
Lemon Cheesecake	36
Brownies	38
Air Fry Churros	39
Vanilla Peanut Butter Cake	41
Classic Apple Fritters	42

MoCho Cake	44
Peanut Butter Banana Bites	46
Caramelized Peaches	47
Watermouth Strawberry Rhubarb Tarts	49
Honey Hazelnut Apples	51
Fruity Oreo Muffins	53
Marshmallow Pastries	55
Chocolate Muffins	57
Cinnamon Apple Crisp	59
Blueberry Muffins	61
New York Cheesecake	63
Tasty Blueberry Apple Crumble	65
Air Fried Apple Pie	67
Fried Peaches	69
Almond Creamy Pudding	71
Baked Peaches And Blueberries	72
Cinnamon Toasted Almonds	73
Mixed Berries With Pecan Streusel	74
Sweetie Cherry Apple Risotto	76
Apple Dumplings	78
Coconut Chocolate Fondue	79
Blueberry Apple Crumble	81
Classic Cinnamon Rolls	83
Baked Plums	85
Air Fryer Banana Muffins	86

Biscuit Donuts	87
Buttered Dinner Rolls	89
Campfire S'mores Banana Boats	91
Eggless Brownies	93
Delicious Beet Root Pudding	95
Easy Doughnuts	97
Sweetie Cranberry Apple Rice Pudding	98
Apricot Crumble With Blackberries	100
Pear And Apple Clafoutis	101
Cookie Custards	103
Creamy Almond And Cardamom Tapioca Pudding	104
Apple Wedges With Apricots	106
Vortex Functions	108

Introduction

My favorite appliance is the Instant Vortex Air Fryer Oven because it's really easy to use. I can cook any kind of food in this oven and there are a lot of features that make cooking easier for me, like preset functions for different types of meat or vegetables. It also cooks evenly so my dish comes out perfect every time! And washes up really easy, unlike other appliances I have used.

This is my favorite appliance because of how easy it makes eating healthier meals possible. There are so many different functions that you can use based on what type of food you're cooking and the end result always comes out better than if you cooked it in a traditional oven or microwave! The best feature this has is how fast the heat circulates throughout the entire unit, it's quickly superheated which cooks your food perfectly every time. Also love how easily the parts come apart for cleaning!

Do you find it hard to decide what to cook? You can buy a kit

specially made for cooking one type of meal, or order meat and vegetables from your favorite restaurant. Both are easy and quick! Resaurant food is bad for your health because it has too much sodium in it, which leads to high blood pressure. And with the kits there's no opportunity at all for creativity - but that might not be such as big deal if you're having trouble deciding what dish should come next on your culinary journey.

The kits will be really nice for people who aren't fans of trying new things, but who just want to stick with the same old thing. If you don't know how to cook, the kit is going to be great for you. You can buy it as a gift for someone else too! The best part about getting someone a cooking kit is that they're going to think of you when they use it and eat their delicious meal...which will be prepared by you!

Cooking your own food at home is a good idea because you can control what ingredients go into it. You can make the food and use easy recipes so that cooking doesn't take up much of your time, using tools like an Instant Vortex to save even more!

Breakfasts, lunch, appetizers and desserts. You can make

them if you are a meat eater or vegetarian. There is something

for everyone here.

The best part of these recipes is that you can make them as

healthy or unhealthy as you want. You might be very hungry

when reading the recipe, but don't worry. You can eat the foods in moderation while still enjoying them.

Of course, if you are vegetarian or vegan there are plenty of options for you too!

I love how easy these recipes are! There isn't anything on a complicated level here at all. You can even get your kids involved with cooking so they aren't eating junk food all the time when they go over friends' houses.

Whether you're a meat eater or vegetarian, there is something

You'll crave. These recipes are for everyone!

The truth is...

This book is not for people who are too careful with their food. It can teach you that it's okay to eat some things you like, but if you're on a diet there may be tips in the book that will help you.

If the diet says so then go ahead and have a cheat day! You can enjoy your favorite foods without feeling guilty because at least they were pre-approved by someone else - or maybe just talk yourself into believing what others say about them being healthy enough? Let's move onto see how this air fryer oven tastes.

it's A MUST have!

This will become one of your favorite kitchen appliances in no time. It's also tiny and won't take up much counter space at all so it'll be nice to keep it out displaying with pride rather than hidden away from sight. I also don't feel like this is going to break down on me anytime soon. I've already dropped the air fryer oven accidentally on my hardwood floor a few times without any problems whatsoever. The even more impressive part about any model is that the inner basket used for cooking can actually go into the dishwasher which makes cleanup super easy.

I enjoy cooking and creating recipes so much that I do it for a hobby.

My Story

As a child, I was thin. Some foods that were fried tasted really good to me without consideration of how many calories they had in them; for example, onion rings and french fries are two examples of food which can be cooked by frying.

The first time my parents ever let me try something fried when we went out to eat at McDonalds after school one day it scared the hell outta' me! First, I tried chicken

strips that were my favorite. When I tasted them they were

good.

I did not like my food because I couldn't eat what I wanted. Air frying food is better. It is healthier and it tastes better too. Now I cook with an air fryer instead of a deep fryer so that the food tastes better to me as well.

I tried to fry things with air. I saw commercials for these machines, and people always ask me if they work. After I used the Instant Vortex for a little while, I realized that it is a good way to make food. It is easy and quick. You can make small quantities of any kind of food with it.

I wanted to try the air fryer, but I was not sure if it would work. Ever since college when my metabolism slowed down and I started putting on pounds again, life has been tough in more ways than one - so much that losing weight is always at the back of mind. So after reading about this new technique for getting a leaner body without depriving oneself from eating what they want (or deep-frying), curiosity got me into buying an Air Fryer!

At first look, you might think there's no way this small device can cook food with or without all the mess; however as soon as you start cooking your own meals using less oil and fat because of its double fan design which circulates hot air and cooks food evenly and quickly, it is safe to say that this thing works!

I have tested the Air Fryer from cooking chicken wings to shrimp tempura, steaks and even whole chickens - everything came out crispier than how they would normally be if fried on a stove.

This gadget can also help reduce the amount of calories you eat daily because deep-frying your own meals means less oil required in preparation without affecting flavor maybe save up to 99% fat intake just by using this machine (and any other air fryers which are now available) - as much as I love eating and indulging myself in cakes and desserts at times, when life gets heavy there's always that one stubborn pound that won't go away despite all your efforts in working out, so to have an alternative that's healthier and more convenient than having to go through the trouble of frying stuff in a pan or in the oven proved helpful.

However, like with all things you'll encounter on the internet - nyself I have 3 air fryers. Yes, there are already air fryers being sold for as low as only $40 dollars at your local chain store but just because it's cheaper and smaller does not necessarily make it better. The reason why I opted for this type over other brands is mainly due its larger size which allows me to cook bigger meals without having to worry about constantly rearranging ingredients when preparing something new.

I like these foods the most. I usually eat them when we go out

to a restaurant. But now that I am getting older, I know that

this is not good for me anymore.

 I got fat. It was hard to lose weight. I know that you need to

give up the things you love to eat. So, I ate less often at

restaurants and gave away my deep-fryer in order to get more control over what I ate.

I did not enjoy my food because I could not eat what I wanted.

One day, I tried to fry things with air. I saw commercials for these machines. People always ask me if they work.

I was a little confused about the air fryer. It can cook food without all the mess. I wanted to try it anyway, but I was not sure if it would work.

I was scared to try it, but I tried it anyway. First, I tried chicken strips that were my favorite. When I tasted them they were good.

Air frying food is good because it tastes as good as food cooked with oil. It is less bad for me, and the food tastes better to me too. I like this way of cooking, so now I cook with air fryer.

After I used the Instant Vortex for a little while, I realized that it was a good way to make food. It is easy and quick. You can make small quantities of any kind of food with it.

When my kids were little, I always cooked for them. Now that I am the only one in the household on a regular basis; it is nice to have an air fryer around which creates great tasting food quickly and conveniently.

Have you ever wanted to make a delicious meal while camping? The Instant Vortex will help you do it without the need of any complicated recipes. This machine can be used for making spaghetti, oatmeal, and even cake! You'll have your favorite food no matter where you are with this device in tow.

Wondering if your food is going to burn or not? With the Digital Air Fryer you won't have any worries about that because you can watch the control panel in front of you. It allows you to keep an eye on things while making sure your food cooks thoroughly and evenly. On top of that, it uses far less oil than a regular deep fryer! So go ahead and make some delicious pankcakes with this product! They'll taste amazing and they won't be too greasy either.

Why You Shoul Buy An Air Fryer or...a Vortex

This book is for everyone. It has many recipes and tips for cooking and creativity. If you are new to cooking, this book has many good recipes to make. More experienced cooks might find some new take on the classics that they have been making for years.

These recipes are healthy and good for you. They can make a quick meal. Fast food is expensive, but this is cheaper and it's good.

1. Instant Vortex is good for healthy and cheap food.

2. Instant Vortex is better for you than regular frying.

Deep fried foods have a lot of calories. There are 9 calories in each gram of fat from deep fried foods. This can make it hard to keep your calories low, but you can still eat deep fried food if you want to and make smarter choices in the rest of what you eat.

The instant vortex is magical because it makes you lose weight by reducing the number of calories you eat.

3. Instant Vortex is a good way to clean your kitchen. You do not need many dishes. You can put it in the air fryer and then cook with a few bowls, so you do not need any big pots or pans.

4. The Vortex has no limits. You can make anything that you would usually cook in an oven, like appetizers for parties like fried cheese sticks, main dishes such as honey baked ham, and desserts like chocolate cakes. Instant Vortex helps you make easy and healthy recipes. It is a new way to think about food--quick and good for your body.

5. All in One Appliance has a way to cook food with air, fry food, broil food and bake it. There is also a rotisserie-style cooking button.

Like Michelangelo...

I love Instant Vortex because it is easy to make. I can also be an artist! This recipe has few ingredients and there are not many steps. But what's best, the book inspires me to cook food that I like too!

We all want to save time and money when cooking. The recipes in this book will help you do just that! You can easily adjust the ingredients for each recipe depending on how much or little food your need, making Instant Vortex a truly versatile appliance.

I don't know if it's the same for you, but in my house, we still celebrate the birthdays of children and the elderly, because there is nothing more beautiful than being able to say to someone: "Thank you for being born, thank you for being close to me.

DO YOU WANT TO KNOW WHY BREAKFAST, WELL I WOULD SAY ALSO BREAKFAST?

I am always cooking dessert at my house and I cook these recipes both breakfast and desserts…it depends from my mood… When there is a guest of honor, I make that dessert for them. I change the shape and color of the desserts depending on who is coming. And I make lots so people can have some to take home if they cannot come to my house.

WHAT IS THIS BOOK ABOUT?

This is a book about desserts. I am just one of those who believe that at the time of birth, no matter [IF] it is that of a child or an adult, we must offer them something sweet and tasty. This kind of idea is not new: after all, for centuries our ancestors have followed this custom without anyone grumbling.

WHO IS IT FOR?

I wrote DESSERTS AND BREAKFAST AIR FRYER COOKBOOK because I'm sure there are many people like me who love to cook desserts and offer them to their guests and relatives. If you're one of these people, then you are in luck because now you don't have to worry here the best selection of desserts recipes will be found under your fingertips!

WHAT'S INSIDE?

I have created a list of dessert and breakfast recipes that you will surely enjoy in privacy of your home kitchen. Each recipe has been tested and written with the utmost accuracy for the best results. Happy cooking, everyone!

Let's Start Creating!

Lemon-Raspberry Muffins

Servings: 6   Prep Time 10 Min   Cooking Time: 15 Minutes

Ingredients:

2 cups almond flour

½ cup coconut oil

½ cup raspberries

¾ cup Swerve

1¼ teaspoons baking powder

⅓ teaspoon ground allspice

⅓ teaspoon ground anise star

½ teaspoon grated lemon zest

¼ teaspoon salt 2 eggs

1 cup sour cream

Directions:

In a bowl, mix almond flour, sugar substitute, baking powder, allspice, anise seed and lemon zest. In another bowl, beat the eggs and add the sour cream and coconut oil. Add this egg mixture to the flour mixture in the first bowl. Stir well to combine them.

Mix in the raspberries. Take the batter out of the bowl. Put three-quarters of it into a muffin pan. Bake for 15 minutes at 345°F in Rack Position 1.

When the cooking is done, the tops of the muffins should be golden and a toothpick should come out clean. Allow the muffins to cool for 10 minutes before taking them out of their pan and serving.

Nutrition:Calories: 245 Protein: 2g   Carbs: 22g   Fat: 18g

Fluffy Brownies Muffins

Serves: 12

Prep Time: 10 mins. Cooking Time: 10 mins.

Ingredients

¼ cup of walnuts, chopped

1 package fudge brownie mix

1 egg

2 teaspoons of water

1/3 cup of vegetable oil

Directions

Set the Instant Vortex on Air fryer to 325 degrees F for 10 minutes. Combine fudge brownie mix with all other ingredients in a bowl. Pour this mixture into 12 muffin molds and place them on the cooking tray. Insert the cooking tray in the Vortex when it displays "Add Food".

Remove from the oven when cooking time is complete. Serve warm.

Nutrition:Calories: 245 Protein: 2.8g   Carbs: 36.9g   Fat: 9.6g

Peanut Butter Custard

Serves: 10
Prep Time: 10 mins. Cooking Time: 21 mins.

Ingredients

4 whole eggs

4 egg yolks

½ cup of granulated sugar ¼ teaspoon of salt 4 cups of whole milk

1 cup of whipping cream

2 teaspoons of vanilla extract 1 cup of caramel

8 tablespoons of peanut butter, smoothened

Directions

Set the air fryer to 350 degrees for 15 minutes. Combine peanut butter with sugar, salt, milk, vanilla extract, eggs and egg yolks in a saucepan. Cook for about 6 minutes on medium-high heat and transfer it to a baking dish.

Put the baking dish on the cooking tray. Put the food in it when it says "Add Food". Take it out when you are done cooking. Mix whipped cream with caramel in a different bowl and serve with peanut butter custard.

Nutrition:Calories: 277 Protein: 11.1g Carbs: 21.9g   Fat: 17.3g

Cinnamon Cheesecake Bars

Servings: 12   Prep Time: 15 Min   Cooking Time: 30 Minutes

Ingredients:

Nonstick cooking spray 16 oz. cream cheese, soft 1 tsp vanilla

1 ¼ cups sugar, divided

2 tubes refrigerated crescent rolls 1 tsp cinnamon

¼ cup butter

Directions:

To make the food, place the rack in position. Spray the bottom of an 8x11-inch pan with cooking spray. In a medium bowl, beat cream cheese, vanilla, and ¾ cup sugar until smooth.

Put a can of crescent rolls on the bottom of the pan. Press them against the sides. Spread cream cheese over the top, but not all over. Put another can of crescent rolls on top and push it into place.

In a bowl, mix together the cinnamon and sugar. Put butter in the oven that is set to 375 degrees for 35 minutes. Sprinkle the cinnamon sugar over the buttery crescents and put some more butter on top if you want.

After the oven has preheated for 5 minutes, put the pan in and then bake for 30 minutes. Make sure it is golden brown, and then take it out. Cool completely. Cover it for at least 2 hours before slicing into pieces and serving.

Nutrition: Calories 336 Fat 18g Carbs 35g Protein 5g

Butter Cake

Serves: 4
Prep Time: 15 mins. Cooking Time: 15 mins.

Ingredients

1 egg

1 2/3 cups of all-purpose flour 1 pinch of salt, or to taste

6 tablespoons of milk

Cooking spray

7 tablespoons of butter, at room temperature

1/4 cup + 2 tablespoons of white sugar

Directions

Put the fryer on 350 degrees F for 15 minutes. Put sugar, flour, and salt in a bowl. Put butter, eggs, and milk in another bowl. Combine sugar mixture with butter mixture. Grease a cake pan with cooking spray and pour cake batter into the cake pan.

You need to put the pan on the cooking tray. Put the cooking tray in when it says "Add Food". Take out of oven when time is up. Eat warm.

Nutrition:Calories: 482 Protein: 7.9g   Carbs: 59.7g   Fat: 22.4g

Oatmeal Cake

Servings: 8   Prep Time: 15 Min   Cooking Time: 40 Minutes

Ingredients:

2 eggs, beaten

1 tbsp cocoa powder 1/2 tsp salt

1 tsp baking soda

1/2 cup butter, softened 1 cup granulated sugar 1 cup brown sugar

1 3/4 cups flour 1 cup quick oats

3/4 cup mix nuts, chopped 2 cups chocolate chips

1 3/4 cup boiling water

Directions:

Take the Instant Vortex oven out of its box. Put it on a rack in position 1. Mix boiling water with oats and butter in a bowl, then add sugar and salt. Add flour, baking soda, cocoa powder, some chocolate chips and nuts. Then put an egg in the mix.

Mix the ingredients together. Spread the batter on a greased cake pan. Sprinkle chocolate chips and nuts over it. Bake at 350 degrees for 45 minutes (or until a toothpick comes out clean). Take it out after 5 minutes and put it in the oven. Slice and serve!

Nutrition: Calories 703 Fat 30.6 g Carbs 97.9 g Protein 64.8 g

Shortbread Fingers

Serves: 10

Prep Time: 20 mins. Cooking Time: 12 mins.

Ingredients

1/3 cup of caster sugar

1 2/3 cups of plain flour 3/4 cup of butter

Directions

Set the Instant Vortex to 355 degrees. Mix the sugar and flour together. Add some butter and mix it up to form a dough. Make 10 pieces of dough and poke them with a fork before putting them in the oven.

When the cooking tray is in the oven, look for "Add food" and put it in. Look for "Turn food" and flip it. And when time is up, take it out of the oven. Serve it while still warm.

Nutrition: Calories: 230 Protein: 2.3g   Carbs: 22.6g   Fat: 14g

Lemon Cheesecake

Serves: 8 Prep Time: 15 mins. Cooking Time: 25 mins.

Ingredients

1 tablespoon of fresh lemon zest, finely grated

2 tablespoon of fresh lemon juice

3 eggs

3 tablespoons of corn starch 2 teaspoons of vanilla extract

17.6-ounces of ricotta cheese

¾ cup of sugar

Directions

Put the air fryer to 320 degrees for 25 minutes. Put eggs in a bowl with other ingredients. Pour mixture into a baking dish and put it on the cooking tray inside the air fryer.

Put the cooking tray in the oven when it says "Add Food". Flip the side of the oven when it says "Turn Food". Take out of the oven when cooking time is done. Serve warm or cold depending on what you want to do with it. Put it in the fridge for 3 hours, serve chilled

Nutrition: Calories: 196 Protein: 9.2g   Carbs: 25.7g   Fat: 6.6g

Brownies

Serves: 10   Prep Time: 10 mins.   Cooking Time: 21 mins.

Ingredients:

½ cup condensed milk

1 tbsp. unsalted butter

2 tbsp. water

½ cup chopped nuts

3 tbsp. melted dark chocolate

1 cup all-purpose flour

Directions:

Add all the ingredients together and mix it well. You will need to grease a pan with butter to put the mixture in. Heat your fryer for five minutes at 300 degrees Fahrenheit. Put the pan in and cover it.

Put a knife or toothpick in the brownies. When they are done, take them out of the oven and eat them with ice cream.

Nutrition: Calories: 243 Protein: 2.8g   Carbs: 36.9g   Fat: 9.6g

Air Fry Churros

Serves: 2 Prep Time: 10mins. Cooking Time: 10 mins.

Ingredients

2 tablespoons of granulated sugar

1/4 teaspoon of salt

1 cup of all-purpose flour

1 cup of water

1/3 cup of unsalted butter, cubed 2 large eggs

1 teaspoon of vanilla extract oil spray

CINNAMON-SUGAR COATING:

1/2 cup of granulated sugar

3/4 teaspoon of ground cinnamon

Directions

Put the Instant Vortex on Air fryer at 375 degrees for 12 minutes. Make a sugar, butter, and salt mixture in a pan with water over medium-high heat. Then mix flour into it and stir it so that it turns into dough. Add vanilla extract to the dough along with eggs that you have mixed with an electric hand mixer

First mix up the ingredients. Then put it in a bag that has a star-shaped tip. Put the mixture on the baking mat and put it in the fridge for an hour. After that, place it on the tray and cook it!

When it says "Add Food", put the cooking tray in. When it says "Turn Food", turn the sides of the cooking tray. Take out when time is up and serve warm.

Nutrition:Calories: 628 Protein: 12.9g Carbs: 61.1g   Fat: 36.6g

Vanilla Peanut Butter Cake

Servings: 8 Prep Time: 15 Min   Cooking Time: 30 Minutes

Ingredients:

1 1/2 cups all-purpose flour 1/3 cup vegetable oil

1 tsp baking soda

1/2 cup peanut butter powder 1 tsp vanilla

1 tbsp apple cider vinegar 1 cup of water

1 cup of sugar 1/2 tsp salt

Directions:

Put the oven on a rack in position 2. Put flour, baking soda, peanut butter powder, sugar and salt together in a big bowl. Mix them up together with some oil mixed with water and vinegar inside of another small bowl. Pour that mixture into the flour mixture in the big bowl and stir it until it is all mixed well together

Pour the batter into a cake pan that is greased with butter. Put the cake in an oven for 35 minutes at 350 F. After 5 minutes put it in the oven. Slice and serve.

Nutrition: Calories 267 Fat 1.8 g Carbs 43.2 g Protein 2.6 g

Classic Apple Fritters

Serves: 4
Cooking Time: 15 mins.

Prep Time: 10 mins.

Ingredients:

Fritters

14 oz raspberries

½ cup of confectioner's sugar 1 tablespoon of cinnamon

1 large apple peeled and chopped 1 cup of self-rising flour

1 cup of plain Greek yogurt 2 teaspoons of sugar Glaze

1 cup of confectioner's sugar

2 tablespoons of milk or more, if needed

Directions:

Put the Instant Vortex Air Fryer at 370 degrees F for 15 minutes. Put all the fritter ingredients in a bowl and mix them up to form a dough. Add milk to make it like icing. Divide the dough into four, and put it on the tray that is inside of the air fryer.

Press the fritter balls down. Put in the cooking tray when it says "Add Food." Flip the sides when it says "Turn Food." Take out of oven when cooking time is done. Top with glaze.

Nutrition: Calories: 252 Protein: 14.1g Carbs: 31.4g Fat: 15.7g

MoCho Cake

Servings: 8   Prep Time: 10 Min   Cooking Time: 30 Minutes

Ingredients:

Dry Ingredients:

1½ cups almond flour

½ cup coconut meal

⅔ cup Swerve

1 teaspoon baking powder

¼ teaspoon salt Wet Ingredients:

1 egg

1 stick butter, melted

½ cup hot strongly brewed coffee Topping:

½ cup confectioner's Swerve ¼ cup coconut flour 3 tablespoons coconut oil

1 teaspoon ground cinnamon

½ teaspoon ground cardamom

Directions:

In a small bowl, mix together the almond flour, coconut meal, Swerve, baking powder and salt. In a larger bowl, whisk together the egg and melted butter with coffee until it is smooth. Add the dry mixture to the wet ingredients and stir until they are well mixed.

Put the batter in a pan. Put all of the ingredients for the topping in a bowl. Pour it on top of the batter and cover it with a spatula. Put it on rack position 1, set the temperature to 330 degrees Fahrenheit, and then set time to 30 minutes.

When cooking is done, the cake should bounce back when you press on it. Wait 10 minutes before serving.

Nutrition:Calories: 628 Protein: 12.9g Carbs: 61.1g Fat: 36.6g

Peanut Butter Banana Bites

Serves: 6 Prep Time: 5 mins. Cooking Time: 6 mins.

Ingredients:

6 wonton wrappers

1/2 cup of peanut butter

2 teaspoons of vegetable oil 1 large banana, sliced

Directions:

Put the Instant Vortex on Air fryer to 380 degrees, and then turn it off. Put 1 teaspoon of peanut butter and 1 banana slice in the middle. Make sure that you wet all of the edges with water, and then close it up by sealing both ends with water.

Place the wrappers on the cooking tray and drizzle with oil. Put them in the Vortex. Flip them when it says to. Take them out when it is done cooking. Serve warm!

Nutrition:Calories: 255 Protein: 8.8g   Carbs: 27.9g   Fat: 12.9g

Caramelized Peaches

Servings: 4
Cooking Time: 10 To 13 Minutes
Prep Time: 10 Min

Ingredients:

2 tablespoons sugar

¼ teaspoon ground cinnamon

4 peaches, cut into wedges

Cooking spray

Directions:

Put sugar and cinnamon on the peaches. Spray the air fryer basket with cooking spray. Place the peaches in a single layer in the basket. Sprinkle them with cooking spray again. Put the basket on a baking pan and set it to 350 degrees Fahrenheit for 10 minutes.

After 5 minutes, remove the peaches from the oven and flip them. Return to the oven for 5 more minutes. When they are done cooking, they should be caramelized and ready to eat. If you need to cook them for 3 more minutes, do that too. Remove from the oven when they are finished cooking and let cool for a few minutes and serve.

Nutrition: Calories: 244 Protein: 2.8g Carbs: 36.9g Fat: 9.6g

Watermouth Strawberry Rhubarb Tarts

Serves: 12 Prep Time: 10 mins. Cooking Time: 12 mins.

Ingredients

1-pound of rhubarb, boiled and cut into

½ inch pieces

½ pound of strawberries

¼ cup of crystallized ginger, chopped

Ready made 12 tart shells, short crust

½ cup of honey

½ cup of whipped cream

Directions

Heat the Instant Vortex on Air Fryer to 375 degrees F for 12 minutes. Make a mixture of rhubarb, strawberries, ginger, honey and whipped cream in a bowl. Fill this mixture in the tart shells and place them on the tray that is inside the cooker.

When the cooking tray says "add food," put it in the oven. When the time is up, take the food out of the oven. Serve it when it's warm.

Nutrition: Calories: 165 Protein: 1.6g   Carbs: 26.2g   Fat: 6.2g

Honey Hazelnut Apples

Servings: 4   Prep Time: 15 Cooking Time: 13 Minutes

Ingredients:

1 oz butter

4 apples

2 oz breadcrumbs Zest of 1 orange

2 tbsp chopped hazelnuts 2 oz mixed seeds

1 tsp cinnamon

2 tbsp honey

Directions:

Preheat the oven to 350 degrees. Cut the apples in half and remove the seeds. Make cuts on the skin of the apple to prevent it from breaking when cooking. Put all of the ingredients into a bowl and stuff them into each apple. Cook for 10 minutes, or until done. Sprinkle with chopped hazelnuts before serving.

Nutrition: Calories: 255 Protein: 8.8g   Carbs: 27.9g   Fat: 12.9g

Fruity Oreo Muffins

Serves: 6   Prep Time: 12 mins. Cooking Time: 10 mins.

Ingredients

1 pack of Oreo biscuits, crushed 1 teaspoon of cocoa powder

½ teaspoon of baking powder

1 cup of milk

¼ teaspoon of baking soda

1 banana, peeled and chopped 1 teaspoon of fresh lemon juice

1 apple, peeled, cored and chopped 1 teaspoon of honey

A pinch of ground cinnamon

Directions

Set the Vortex to 325 degrees F for 10 minutes. Put biscuits, cocoa powder, baking soda, milk and baking powder in a bowl. Pour this into 6 muffin molds and place them on the tray when it says "Add Food".

When the cooking time is up, take the muffins out of the oven. Meanwhile, mix together apples, bananas, honey, lemon juice and cinnamon in a bowl. Put this on top of the muffins to serve.

Nutrition:Calories: 185 Protein: 3.1g   Carbs: 31.4g   Fat: 5.9g

Marshmallow Pastries

Servings: 4

Prep Time: 10 Min   Cooking Time: 5 Minutes

Ingredients:

4 phyllo pastry sheets, thawed

2 oz. butter, melted

¼ cup chunky peanut butter

4 teaspoons marshmallow fluff

Pinch of salt

Directions:

Put one sheet of phyllo on the counter. Put another sheet on top of it and put butter on it. Keep doing this until you have four sheets.

Cut the phyllo in strips and put peanut butter and marshmallow fluff on the underside of a strip. Fold over the tip of the sheet so that it makes a triangle, then fold over again in a zigzag manner.

To make something, first press the power button. Then choose the air fry mode and set time to 5 minutes. Next, press the temp button and set it at 360 degrees Fahrenheit. Press start/pause to start cooking.

When the unit beeps, open the oven door and put in a greased "Air Fry Basket." Sprinkle with salt. Serve warm.

Nutrition: Calories 251 Fat 20.5 g   Carbs Protein 5.2 g

Chocolate Muffins

Serves: 12

Prep Time: 10 mins. Cooking Time: 10 mins.

Ingredients

2 medium eggs

5 tablespoons of milk

25 g of cocoa powder

75 g of milk chocolate

200 g of self-rising flour

225 g of caster sugar

100 g of butter

½ teaspoon of vanilla essence

Directions

Set the Instant Vortex on Air fryer to 360 degrees F for 10 minutes. Put in the cocoa, flour, and sugar in a bowl. Mix eggs with milk and vanilla butter in another bowl. Add the mixture of cocoa, flour, and sugar to the eggs with milk mix. Pour mixture into 12 muffin molds.

First put the muffin molds on the baking tray. Then you put the baking tray in the oven when it says "Add food". Remove from oven when cooking time is over. Serve warm.

Nutrition:Calories: 247 Protein: 3g   Carbs: 36g   Fat: 10.2g

Cinnamon Apple Crisp

Servings: 4

Prep Time: 10 Min Cooking Time: 35 Minutes

Ingredients:

1/8 tsp ground clove 1/8 tsp ground nutmeg 2 tbsp honey

4 1/2 cups apples, diced 1 tsp ground cinnamon 1 tbsp cornstarch

1 tsp vanilla 1/2 lemon juice For topping:

1 cup rolled oats

1/3 cup coconut oil, melted 1 tsp cinnamon

1/3 cup honey

1/2 cup almond flour

Directions:

Put the rack into position 2 in the Instant Vortex oven. Put a bowl on it. Mix apples, vanilla, lemon juice and honey together. Sprinkle spices and cornstarch on top and mix well with a spoon.

Pour apple mixture into a baking dish. In a bowl, mix together coconut oil, cinnamon, almond flour, oats and honey. Put the honey mixture on top of the apples. Bake for 40 minutes at 350 F. After 5 minutes put the dish in the oven that is already heated to 350 F. Serve and enjoy!

Nutrition: Calories 450 Fat 21 g Carbs 65 g Protein 4 g

Blueberry Muffins

Serves: 6

Prep Time: 10 mins. Cooking Time: 15 mins.

Ingredients

1 cup of frozen blueberries

1 egg

1/3 cup of coconut sugar

½ teaspoon of salt

2 teaspoons of baking powder

¼ cup of unsweetened applesauce

1 teaspoon of vanilla extract

¼ cup of ghee, melted

1 cup of cassava flour, or your favorite gluten-free flour

¼ cup of unsweetened almond milk

Directions

Set the Instant Vortex on Air fryer to 360 degrees F for 10 minutes. Put coconut sugar, cassava flour, baking powder, and salt in a bowl. Cream together egg, applesauce, ghee (or butter), unsweetened almond milk (or soy or dairy milk), and vanilla extract in another bowl.

Take out 6 muffin molds. Pour the mixture of frozen blueberries and cassava flour into the muffin molds. Put them on the cooking tray, then put it in the oven when it says to add food. Wait until it is finished cooking and then serve them warm.

Nutrition:Calories: 202 Protein: 2.9g   Carbs: 27.5g   Fat: 8.8g

New York Cheesecake

Servings: 8 Prep Time: 20 Min Cooking Time: 15 Minutes

Ingredients:

1 ½ cups almond flour

3 ounces swerve

1/2 stick butter, melted

20 ounces full-fat cream cheese

1/2 cup heavy cream 1 ¼ cups granulated swerve

3 eggs, at room temperature

1 tablespoon vanilla essence

1 teaspoon grated lemon zest

Directions:

On a baking pan, put a little flour. Mix the almond flour and swerve together. Add butter and mix until it looks like breadcrumbs. Spread the mixture on the bottom of the pan to form an even layer. Put in oven for 7 minutes at 330 degrees F until it is golden brown.

Let the food cool on a wire rack. Then, with a mixer, mix together the cheese and cream. Add some sugar. Mix until it is creamy and fluffy.

Break the eggs into a bowl. Add vanilla and lemon zest. Mix until combined. Put the topping on top of the pie crust and spread it out evenly.

Bake your cheesecake in the Air Fryer at 330 degrees F for 25 to 30 minutes. Leave it inside the Air Fryer for another 30 minutes after you take it out of the oven. Cover your cheesecake with plastic wrap. Put it in the refrigerator and let it cool 6 hours or overnight. Serve well chilled!

Nutrition: 247 Calories 22g Fat   5g Carbs 8g Protein

Tasty Blueberry Apple Crumble

Serves: 6 Prep Time: 5 mins. Cooking Time: 15 mins.

Ingredients:

1 medium apple, finely diced

1/2 cup of frozen blueberries strawberries

2/3 cup of rice flour

2 tablespoons of sugar

1/2 teaspoon of ground cinnamon

2 tablespoons of nondairy butter

Directions:

Set the Instant Vortex on Air fryer to 350 degrees for 15 minutes. Put apples and blueberries in a bowl. Put butter, flour, cinnamon and sugar in another bowl. Pour the butter mixture into the apple mixture and stir it with a spoon. Put it on the cooking tray, then put it into the air fryer for 15 minutes.

When the Vortex says "Add Food," put the cooking tray on it. When the Vortex says "Turn Food," turn upside down. When cooking time is done, take out of oven and serve.

Nutrition:Calories: 377 Protein: 5.2g   Carbs: 23.7g   Fat: 29.7g

Air Fried Apple Pie

Serves: 6
Cooking Time: 30 mins.

Prep Time: 10 mins.

Ingredients:

1 large apple, chopped

2 teaspoons of lemon juice

1 tablespoon of ground cinnamon 1 pie crust, refrigerated

Baking spray

½ teaspoon of vanilla extract

1 tablespoon of butter

1 beaten egg

1 tablespoon of raw sugar

2 tablespoons of sugar

Directions:

Set the Instant Vortex on Air fryer to 350 degrees F for 30 minutes. Split the pie crust into two halves and spread it into a greased pan. Combine apple with sugar, cinnamon, lemon juice, and vanilla extract in a bowl. Fill the pie crust with the apple mixture and cover with a half of the pie crust.

Put some egg on the top of the pie. Sprinkle some sugar on it. Put it in the oven when you see "Add Food". Turn it around when you see "Turn Food". Take it out when you see "Cooking Time Complete."

Nutrition:Calories: 371 Protein: 7.2g   Carbs: 72.8g   Fat: 6g

Fried Peaches

Servings: 4   Prep Time: 5 Min   Cooking Time: 15 Minutes

Ingredients:

4 ripe peaches (1/2 a peach = 1 serving)

1 1/2 cups flour

Salt

2 egg yolks

3/4 cups cold water

1 1/2 tablespoons olive oil

2 tablespoons brandy

4 egg whites Cinnamon/sugar mix

Directions:

Mix the ingredients together in a bowl. Add water and brandy. Put it in the fridge for 2 hours. Bring a pot of water to a boil. Cut an X at the bottom of each peach and place them in the boiling water for 30 seconds on each side, then transfer them to the ice bath for 45 seconds.

Boil each peach for a minute. Then it will be hard to peel. Put the peels in the ice water. Beat egg whites with a mixer and put into batter mix. Dip each peach into the batter to coat it and fry on the stove or in an air fryer until done.

Cook at 360 degrees for 10 Minutes. Prepare a plate with cinnamon/sugar mix, roll peaches in the mix and serve.

Nutrition: calories 306 fat 5.3g   protein 10g   Carbs 8.7g

Almond Creamy Pudding

Serves: 6   Prep Time: 15 mins. Cooking Time: 30 mins.

Ingredients

4 cups of whole milk 3 packets stevia

1 teaspoon of instant espresso powder 1 teaspoon of vanilla extract

2 cups of almond meal

1 teaspoon of ground cinnamon

Directions

Put the Instant Vortex on Air fryer on to be at 350 degrees for 30 minutes. Mix almond meal, milk, stevia, cardamom, cinnamon and vanilla extract in a saucepan. Add this to the baking dish with a spoon. Put it in the cooking tray when it says "Add Food". Remove from oven when cooking time is complete.

Nutrition:Calories: 286 Protein: 12g   Carbs: 21.8g   Fat: 15.7g

Baked Peaches And Blueberries

Servings: 6   Prep Time: 10 Min   Cooking Time: 10 Minutes

Ingredients:

3 peaches, peeled, halved, and pitted

2 tablespoons packed brown sugar

1 cup plain Greek yogurt

¼ teaspoon ground cinnamon

1 teaspoon pure vanilla extract

1 cup fresh blueberries

Directions:

Put the peaches in the pan with their cut side up. Put brown sugar on them. Slide the pan into position 1 and set it to 380 degrees for 10 minutes.

Meanwhile, mix the yogurt, vanilla and cinnamon in a bowl. Put this on the stove to cook. When cooking is done, take it out of the oven to put it on your plate. Serve with blueberries on top.

Nutrition: Calories: 381 Protein: 5.2g   Carbs: 23.7g   Fat: 29.7g

Cinnamon Toasted Almonds

Serves: 6　　　　　　　　　　　Prep Time: 15 mins. Cooking Time: 45 mins.

Ingredients:

1 teaspoon of cold water 2 packets of stevia

1 egg white

¼ teaspoon of salt

½ teaspoon of ground cinnamon

4 cups of whole almonds

Directions:

Put the Instant Vortex on the Air fryer at 250 degrees Fahrenheit for 45 minutes. Add egg whites to a bowl with water and whip it until frothy. Add cinnamon, nuts, stevia, and salt into the egg whites and fold them together until they are mixed well. Make sure that you put this mixture onto a baking tray.

When your Vortex is telling you to add food, put the cooking tray in. When it tells you to turn food, flip the sides. When it is done cooking, take it out and serve it warm.

Nutrition:Calories: 372 Protein: 14.4g Carbs: 14g　Fat: 31.7g

Mixed Berries With Pecan Streusel

Servings: 3 Prep Time: 12 Min Cooking Time: 15 Minutes

Ingredients:

3 tablespoons pecans, chopped

3 tablespoons almonds, slivered

2 tablespoons walnuts, chopped

3 tablespoons granulated swerve

1/2 teaspoon ground cinnamon

1 egg

2 tablespoons cold salted butter, cut into pieces

1/2 cup mixed berries

Directions:

First, mix the nuts, and cinnamon together with some butter. Mix it up! Then add eggs to the mix. Pour the berries on the bottom of an Air Fryer-safe dish and then put your nut mixture on top of that. Bake this at 340°F for 17 minutes at room temperature (not hot).

Nutrition : Calories 257 Fat 28g Carbs 1g Protein 3g

Sweetie Cherry Apple Risotto

Serves: 4

Prep Time: 10 mins. Cooking Time: 12 mins.

Ingredients

1 tablespoon of butter

¼ cup of brown sugar

½ cup of apple juice

1½ cups of milk

¾ cup of Arborio rice, boiled

1 apple, diced

2 pinches salt

¾ teaspoon of cinnamon powder

¼ cup of dried cherries

1½ tablespoons of almonds, roasted and sliced

¼ cup of whipped cream

Directions

Put the cooking tray on top of the Instant Vortex Air fryer. Press 375 degrees F. Add butter, sugar, apple juice, milk, apple, salt, and cinnamon to the rice. Put the rice in a bowl and pour it into the cooking tray that is on top of your Instant Vortex Air fryer set to 375 degrees F

Put the cooking tray in the oven when it wants to put food in. When it tells you to turn the food, you should too. When cooking is done, take out from oven and put cherries, almonds, and whipped cream on top.

Nutrition:Calories: 320 Protein: 6.2g   Carbs: 54.8g   Fat: 8.5g

Apple Dumplings

Servings: 4   Prep Time: 10 Min Cooking Time: 25 Minutes

Ingredients:

2 tbsp. melted coconut oil

2 puff pastry sheets

1 tbsp. brown sugar

2 tbsp. raisins

2 small apples of choice

Directions:

Preparing the ingredients. First, make sure your air fryer oven is preheated to 356 degrees. Next, peel and core the apples. Then mix in raisins and sugar. Place a bit of apple mixture into puff pastry sheets and brush the sides with melted coconut oil.

Air fry. Put into the Instant Vortex air fryer. Cook for 25 minutes, turning halfway through. When it is done it will be golden.

Nutrition: Calories: 368 Fat:7g   Protein:3g Carbs:5g

Coconut Chocolate Fondue

Serves: 4   Prep Time: 10 mins. Cooking Time: 5 mins.

Ingredients

2 teaspoons of sugar

2 teaspoons of coconut essence

200 g of Swiss bittersweet chocolate (70%)

2 teaspoons of coconut milk powder

2 cups of water

200 g of coconut cream

Directions

In the Instant Vortex Air fryer, set it to 375 degrees F for 8 minutes. Mix chocolate with coconut cream and sugar and put it in the ramekin.

Put the ramekin on the cooking tray. Put the tray in the Vortex when it says to. When it is done, take it out of the oven. Add coconut essence to taste and stir in coconut milk powder by adding more water and heating until smooth. Serve in a fondue pot.

Nutrition: Calories: 268 Protein: 2.8g   Carbs: 16.8g   Fat: 21.4g

Blueberry Apple Crumble

Servings: 6   Prep Time: 15 Min   Cooking Time: 15 Minutes

Ingredients:

1 medium apple, finely diced

1/2 cup of frozen blueberries strawberries

2/3 cup of rice flour

2 tablespoons of sugar

1/2 teaspoon of ground cinnamon

2 tablespoons of nondairy butter

Directions:

Set the Instant Vortex on Air fryer to 350 degrees. Put apple and blueberries in a bowl. Mix butter, flour, sugar, and cinnamon in another bowl. Put the butter mixture into the apple mixture and mix it together.

Put this mixture on the cooking sheet. Put the cooking sheet in the oven when it shows "add food". Flip the sides when it shows "turn food". Take out of the oven when it is done cooking. Serve warm.

Nutrition: Calories: 377 Fat: 29.7 g Carbs:23.7 g Protein: 5.2 g

Classic Cinnamon Rolls

Serves: 8　　　　　　　　　　Prep Time: 8 mins.　Cooking Time: 7 mins.

Ingredients

Cinnamon rolls:

¾ stick of unsalted butter, softened

1 tablespoon of ground cinnamon

6 tablespoons of brown sugar

1 sheet of puff pastry, thawed Icing:

½ cup of powdered sugar

1 tablespoon of milk

2 teaspoons of fresh lemon juice

Directions

Put the Instant Vortex on Air fryer at 400 degrees F for 7 minutes. Mix butter and sugar with cinnamon in a bowl. Then put it on the middle of the pastry sheet. Roll it well until butter is spread all over. Cut into 1-inch pieces, or as desired.

Place the bread on the tray. Put the tray into the machine when it says "Add Food." Turn the sides when it says "Turn Food." Remove from oven when cooking is done. Mix milk with sugar and lemon juice to make icing. Frost bread with this icing and serve.

Nutrition:Calories: 252 Protein: 2g   Carbs: 22g   Fat: 18g

Baked Plums

Servings: 6 Prep Time: 12 Min   Cooking Time: 20 Minutes

Ingredients:

6 plums, cut into wedges 1 teaspoon ginger, ground

½ teaspoon cinnamon powder Zest of 1 lemon, grated 2 tablespoons water

10 drops stevia

Directions:

In a pan, mix the plums with the other ingredients. Put it in air fryer and cook it at 360 degrees Fahrenheit for 20 minutes. Serve chilled.

Nutrition: Calories 172 Fat 5, Carbs 3, Protein 5

Air Fryer Banana Muffins

Serves: 10

Prep Time: 5 mins. Cooking Time: 15 mins.

Ingredients

1 egg

1 teaspoon of cinnamon

1/2 cup of brown sugar

1 teaspoon of vanilla extract

2 very ripe bananas, mashed

1/3 cup of olive oil

3/4 cup of self-rising flour

Directions

Set the Instant Vortex to 325 degrees F and cook for 15 minutes. Mix mashed banana with egg, brown sugar, olive oil, and vanilla extract in a bowl. Mix flour and cinnamon in another bowl. Add the flour mixture to the banana mixture until it's mixed together well.

Mix the ingredients together. Add the mixture to muffin tins. Place them on an oven tray. Put it in the oven when it says "Add food". Take it out of the oven when it is done cooking.

Meanwhile, mingle apple, banana, honey, lemon juice, and cinnamon in another bowl. Serve with tea.

Nutrition:Calories: 163 Protein: 2g   Carbs: 22g   Fat: 8g

Biscuit Donuts

Serves: 4   Prep Time: 10 mins.
Cooking Time: 5 mins.

Ingredients:

Coconut oil

1 can of biscuit dough, pre-made 1/2 cup of white sugar 1/2 cup of powdered sugar

2 tablespoons of melted butter 2 teaspoons of cinnamon

Directions:

First, put the Instant Vortex on Air fryer to 350 degrees F. Cut the dough with a biscuit cutter. Brush olive oil on the cooking tray and place biscuits on it. Put in the cooking tray when it says "Add Food"

When the oven says "Turn Food", flip the dish so that the other side is up. The doughnuts must be cooked for a certain amount of time and then they are done. When they are done, put butter on them and one of two things: cinnamon or sugar. Serve warm!

Nutrition: Calories: 303   Protein: 8.9g   Carbs: 25g   Fat: 32.2g

Buttered Dinner Rolls

Servings: 12 Prep Time: 15 Min Cooking Time: 30 Minutes

Ingredients:

1 cup milk

3 cups plain flour

7½ tablespoons unsalted butter

1 tablespoon coconut oil

1 tablespoon olive oil

1 teaspoon yeast

Salt and black pepper, to taste

Directions:

Preheat the Air fryer to 360 degree F and grease a cooking pan. Put olive oil, milk, and coconut oil in the pan and cook for 3 minutes. Take the pot of food away from the stove. Mix together plain flour, yeast, butter, salt, and black pepper in a large bowl.

Knead the dough with your hands for about 5 minutes. Keep it covered in a damp cloth and place it somewhere warm. Let it sit there for 30 minutes. After that, knead the dough again for 5 minutes. Keep it covered and put it back where you found the first one to let it sit there for another 30 minutes in a warm place.

Divide the dough into 12 equal pieces and roll each into a ball, arrange 6 balls into the Air fryer basket in a single layer and cook for about 15 minutes. Repeat with the remaining balls and serve warm.

Nutrition: Calories: 209 Fat: 11.3g Carbs: 25g Protein: 4.1g

Campfire S'mores Banana Boats

Serves: 4

Prep Time: 10 mins. Cooking Time: 4 mins.

Ingredients:

4 bananas

3 tablespoons of mini semi-sweet chocolate chips

3 tablespoons of mini marshmallows

3 tablespoons of graham cracker cereal

Aluminum foil

Cooking oil spray

Directions:

Put a pan in the Air fryer. Turn it on. Set it to 350 degrees F for 4 minutes. Put the bananas on an aluminum sheet with cooking oil spray before you put them in the pan. Tear open one side of the banana and stuff it with chocolate chips, marshmallows, and graham cereal.

Cover completely with foil and place on the cooking tray. Insert the cooking tray in the Vortex when it displays "Add Food". Remove from the oven when cooking time is complete. Serve warm.

Nutrition: Calories: 249 Protein: 5g   Carbs: 14.8g   Fat: 11.9g

Eggless Brownies

Servings: 8   Prep Time: 10 Cooking Time: 40 Minutes

Ingredients:

1/4 cup walnuts, chopped

1/3 cup cocoa powder

2 tsp baking powder

1 cup of sugar

1 cup all-purpose flour

1/2 cup chocolate chips

2 tsp vanilla

1 tbsp milk

3/4 cup yogurt

1/2 cup butter, melted

1/4 tsp salt

Directions:

Put the oven rack in position 1. Put flour, cocoa powder, baking powder, and salt in a bowl. Mix well and put aside for later. Stir butter, vanilla, milk, and yogurt together until they are mixed. Add the flour mixture to the butter mixture and mix it together until it is just combined. Then fold in walnuts and chocolate chips.

Pour batter into the prepared baking dish, set to bake at 350 F for 45 minutes. After 5 minutes place the baking dish in the preheated oven. Slice and serve.

Nutrition: Calories 361 Fat 18 g Carbs 48 g Protein 5.5 g

Delicious Beet Root Pudding

Serves: 6   Prep Time: 15 mins. Cooking Time: 15 mins.

Ingredients

18 almonds, peeled

1 teaspoon of cardamom powder

½ cup of condensed milk

1-pound of green beetroot, freshly grated

2 tablespoons of unsalted butter

3 tablespoons of mascarpone cheese

3 tablespoons of whipped cream

½ cup full fat milk

Directions

Set the Instant Vortex on Air fryer to 350 degrees F for 35 minutes. Add beets, garlic powder, salt and pepper, flour, eggs and water. Put everything in a bowl except for the cream and almonds. Pour this mixture into an oven dish.

Put the baking dish on the cooking tray. Put the cooking tray in the oven when it says "Add food!" Take out of oven when it says done. Add almonds and whipped cream to top off pudding.

Nutrition:Calories: 197 Protein: 5.4g   Carbs: 19.3g   Fat: 11.2g

Easy Doughnuts

Servings: 4   Prep Time: 10 Cooking Time: 25 Minutes

Ingredients:

8 oz self-rising flour 1 tsp baking powder

½ cup milk

2 ½ tbsp butter 1 egg

2 oz brown sugar

Directions:

Turn on the oven to 350 degrees Fahrenheit. Beat the butter and sugar until it is smooth. Add the egg and milk and make sure that it is mixed. Mix in flour with baking powder in a bowl, then add the butter mixture from before.

Form donut shapes and cut off the center with cookie cutters. Arrange on a lined baking sheet and cook in for 15 minutes. Serve with whipped cream or icing.

Nutrition: Calories: 303   Protein: 8.8g   Carbs: 25g Fat: 32.2g

Sweetie Cranberry Apple Rice Pudding

Serves: 4   Prep Time: 10 mins. Cooking Time: 12 mins.

Ingredients

¾ cup of Arborio rice, soaked

2 pinches salt

¼ cup of brown sugar

1½ cups of milk

¾ teaspoon of cinnamon powder

½ cup of apple juice

¼ cup of dried cranberries

1½ tablespoons of almonds, roasted and sliced

1 tablespoon of butter

1 apple, diced

¼ cup of whipped cream

Directions

Put the Instant Vortex on Air fryer to 375 degrees F for 12 minutes. Put butter, sugar, apple juice, milk, apple and salt in a bowl. Then put the rice in it. Put this mix into a baking dish. Put the baking dish onto the cooking tray of your Instant Vortex on Air fryer

Add the cooking tray to the Vortex when it says "add food". You should remove it from the oven when time is up. Top with dried cranberries, almonds, and whipped cream before serving.

Nutrition:Calories:318 Protein: 6.1g   Carbs: 54.9g   Fat: 8.5g

Apricot Crumble With Blackberries

Servings: 4   Prep Time: 11 Min   Cooking Time: 30 Minutes

Ingredients:

2 ½ cups fresh apricots, de-stoned and cubed 1 cup fresh blackberries

½ cup sugar

2 tbsp lemon Juice

1 cup flour

5 tbsp butter

Directions:

Turn the oven to 360 F. Put apricots and lemon juice and 2 tbsp sugar into a bowl. Add blackberries. Scoop mixture into a greased dish. Make sure it is even in the dish so that it cooks evenly when you bake it.

In a bowl, mix flour and sugar. Add some butter and water. Mix it until it is crumbly. Cover the fruit mixture with this. Cook for 20 minutes.

Nutrition: Calories: 197   Protein: 5.4g   Carbs: 19.3g   Fat: 11.2g

Pear And Apple Clafoutis

Serves: 8   Prep Time: 10 mins. Cooking Time: 25 mins.

Ingredients:

1 cup of milk

1 tablespoon of vanilla extract

2 tablespoons of powdered sugar

2 cups of water

2 eggs

1 cup of apples, chopped

1 cup of pears, chopped

¾ cup of sugar

2 cups of all-purpose flour Oil, for greasing

Directions:

Put the Instant Vortex on a 375 degree F setting and set it to cook for 8 minutes. Blend together eggs, sugar, vanilla extract, milk and flour in a bowl. Scoop this batter into an oven-safe cake pan. Add chopped pears and apples to the top of the cake batter. Wrap with aluminum foil.

Pour the cake mix in the baking tin. Put it on the cooking tray and put it in the oven when it says "Add Food". Take out of the oven when it is done. Serve warm with tea.

Nutrition: Calories: 252 Protein: 5.8g   Carbs: 52.7g   Fat: 2.1g

Cookie Custards

Serves: 8

Prep Time: 10 mins. Cooking Time: 25 mins.

Ingredients:

2 tbsp. margarine

A pinch of baking soda and baking powder

1 cup all-purpose flour

½ cup icing sugar

½ cup custard powder

Directions:

Cream together the margarine, sugar and all other ingredients. Make balls out of the dough and coat them in flour. Place the balls in a tray that you have greased with butter. Turn on your fryer to 300 Fahrenheit for five minutes.

Put the baking tray in the basket. Cover it with a lid and cook until the balls have turned golden brown. Take out the baking tray, put it on a plate and leave it on your lawn for half an hour to cool. Put them in an airtight container when they are cool enough to be stored away from heat.

Nutrition: Calories 361 Fat 18 g Carbs 47 g Protein 5.5 g

Creamy Almond And Cardamom Tapioca Pudding

Serves: 4

Prep Time: 15 mins. Cooking Time: 12 mins.

Ingredients:

1 cup of whole milk

½ cup of sugar

50 g of tapioca pearls

½ teaspoon of cardamom powder

½ cup of almonds, roasted

½ cup of water

Directions:

To set the Instant Vortex on Air fryer, use 375 degrees for 12 minutes. Put tapioca pearls in a bowl with milk and sugar. Add cardamom powder and water. Pour the mixture into a baking dish.

Place the baking dish on the cooking tray. Put the cooking tray into the Vortex when it says "Add Food". Take out of oven when time is up. Put almonds on top.

Nutrition: Calories: 243 Protein: 4.5g   Carbs: 41.6g   Fat: 7.9g

Apple Wedges With Apricots

Servings: 4   Prep Time: 8 Min   Cooking Time: 15 To 18 Minutes

Ingredients:

4 large apples, peeled and sliced into 8 wedges

2 tablespoons olive oil

½ cup dried apricots, chopped

1 to 2 tablespoons sugar

½ teaspoon ground cinnamon

Directions:

Toss the apple wedges with a bit of olive oil in a bowl. Put them into the air fryer basket, then put it on your baking pan and slide it into Rack Position 2. Set the temperature to 350°F and set time to 15 minutes.

After 12 minutes, take the apples out of the oven. Sprinkle on some apricots and then air fry for 3 more minutes. In the meantime, mix together sugar and cinnamon in a bowl until it is smooth. Take the apple wedges off of the oven to a plate. Then sprinkle on some sugar mixture before you serve them.

Nutrition:Calories: 242 Protein: 2.8g   Carbs: 36.9g   Fat: 9.6g

Vortex Functions

The smart programs are automated. They are programmed

to do things like set the time or temperature. When you usethese functions you never need to set them yourself. Whenthe oven goes into standby mode, it will display "OFF". Thesesmart programs are:

Different Smart Programs/Function Modes

1. Air Fry
2. Broil
3. Roast
4. Bake
5. Dehydrate
6. Reheat

The Vortex Air Fryer Oven comes with a touch screen LEDdisplay and various functions that are used during the Thevortex air f ryer has a touch panel that is digital. You can use itto cook your food automatically or manually.

StartThe Start button is used to start the cooking process.As the name suggests, when you press cancel, it will stop yourcooking. When you press cancel, it will stop your cooking andthen go on standby mode.LightYou can use the (+ / -) time button to change the cooking timeon your stove. To increase cooking time, touch and hold "+". Todecrease cooking time, touch and hold "-".Rotate(+ / -) Temperature Controls (Temp)The (+) button is used to make the temperature higher andthe (-) button is used to make the temperature lower.(+ / -) TimeThe Light button is used to turn ON and OFF the oven light.After 5 minutes of time oven light turn OFF automatically.Cancel

When you start the cooking process, the Rotate button willturn on. You just need to touch it once more to stop therotisserie. This button is only available when you choose Air Fryor Roast in the cooking process. When the key turns blue, thenit means that you can use it.

Desserts Breakfast Air Fryer Cookbook

www.ingramcontent.com/pod-product-compliance
Lightning Source LLC
Chambersburg PA
CBHW081417080526
44589CB00016B/2577